Offerings
to
Pilgrims

Offerings to Pilgrims

Carroll Blair

Aveon Publishing Company

ISBN: 978-1-936430-36-9

Library of Congress Control Number
2011903871

Aveon Publishing Co.
P.O. Box 380739
Cambridge, MA 02238-0739 USA

Also by Carroll Blair

Grains of Thought
Facing the Circle
Reel to Real
Shifting Tides
Reaches
Out of Silence
Quarter Notes
By Rays of Light
Into the Inner Life
Gnosis of the Heart
Soul Reflections
Beneath and Beyond the Surface
Of Courage and Commitment
For Today and Tomorrow
In Meditation
Sightings Along the Journey
Through Desert's Fire
Human Natures
(Of Animal and Spiritual)
Atoms from the Suns of Solitude
Colors of Devotion
Voicings
Through the Shadows
As the World Winds Flow

If what you are reading now is
keeping you from communing
with your own thoughts, then
close this book and go to them,
for nothing is more important
for you and your future
than what is flowering within.
One can never know what
wonders may be blossoming.

Finding your spiritual voice is synonymous with finding your life.

Everything is rooted inside, to be neglected, or nurtured and realized.

To follow anyone or anything is to only prepare you to one day follow yourself . . . (your higher self).

True progress is an individual affair, achieved in individual lives, one step at a time.

The daily goals of the enlightened harmonize with the goals of their lives.

Whatever one does, whatever one's time and energy are given to, should not the question always be "Is this fruitful?"

The face of your tomorrow is created
by the sculpting of your today.

When you bring all your power and
attention to the moment, the power
of Life is there to greet you.

It is impossible to not be creative
when experiencing the fullness
of the moment.

The world has seen every manifest
of wealth but your inner wealth.

There is always originality to be mined
in any serious quest for enlightenment.

You carry the search with you, for it is
within you.

Truth, beauty, wisdom . . . of these
that are earnestly sought, the seeker
joins with and draws from.

The crux of the spiritual life is its
focus, lived with a growing realization
of purpose.

To have faith in your mission is to
be able to endure, though no one else
would have faith in you.

When the inner light is strong enough, radiant enough, all the darkness of the world cannot veil it in shadow.

For something to have an effect on you requires your participation.

Know that whatever may trouble you in the goings-on of the day-to-day is of the fleeting, therefore of illusion, as phantoms rising and falling like chimerical dust.

To be open to all things doesn't mean to
allow entry to all things.

One can arm oneself in no better way
against the follies of the world than by
fostering a keen awareness of one's follies.

The wise concentrate on what they need
to develop that will enable them to need
less.

Part of wisdom is knowing when to
save one's energies and when to spend
them, and what to spend them on.

There are more slaveries to choose
from in life than there are freedoms.

If you were placed in a large room that
you couldn't leave, would you prefer the
area to be spacious, or fully occupied?
To be mobile-friendly, or littered with
nonessentials, severely limiting your
movements? Now imagine this room
to be the universe of your life.

Before one can make something of
oneself one must know what he or she
is made of — (and this cannot be done
in a crowded house).

A spiritual DNA is as unique as a
DNA of the physical.

To know yourself goes far beyond
how you think or feel about yourself.

To find your way to the world that is you, you must go to where nothing of the world can reach you.

Solitude has everything to do with inner being, nothing to do with what is or isn't outside of you.

There needs to be work on one's life before the work of one's life can proceed with efficiency.

As much to do with what one has is
what one hasn't in being equipped to
carry out the performance of something.

A life cannot operate through light
that is weighed down with the trivial.

Observe the ratio of space to matter.
Does this not mirror how fundamental
the greater abundance of space is to the
creation of the whole?

How often it is that what someone
believes he cannot live without today
is hardly a memory tomorrow.

Preoccupation with the worldly is a
kind of poverty. Freedom from it is
a wealth.

To go with the fashion-flow is counterproductive
to the industry of internal growth, the former
leading away from depth creation and the
realization of human potential.

Between sloth and eagerness there is
much to cloud the way to spiritualization.

Who seeks the lasting will not find it in
ego flatteries and earthly gains, for such
can only fill the innocent with delusions
and distract the spiritual aspirant from
the true mission of growth and discovery
of the eternal within.

Enlightenment turns away from the
coming and going, looking to what
is always.

What draws one closer to Life, inspiring
a sense of wonder and appreciation, is of
the good. Not so, what does the opposite.

Emanation of the transcendent always shines
through, and is always beautiful.

The truly outstanding is not what stands
out in the crowd, but what is standing
outside of it.

The world is what it is from moment
to moment, but you have a choice of
what that moment will be for you.

In life there are many things to
understand or be understood, but
of Life, there is only to experience.

Love is where it begins.

A spiritual life isn't all about the spiritual looking out for one; it is also about one looking out for the spiritual — (i.e., honoring it, defending it, giving it the reverence that it deserves).

The way to completeness is by way of gratitude.

A sunny morning, and the birds sing their songs. A damp, cloud-filled morning, and the birds are singing their beautiful songs.

The makeup of a day has nothing
to do with what one makes of it.

When one brings beauty to something
observed that is beautiful, the joy
of the experience is enhanced.

There is not love without inner light,
nor inner light without love.

What death cannot take knows the language of silence.

The calm of wisdom is like the fire of the hearth — self-contained warmth untouched by passing winds of the temporal.

One need not go on some retreat to "get away from it all" . . . one can retire at any moment into the sanctum of inner-being to be reminded of what is real, and the importance of staying connected to it.

The thread of any life cannot be broken,
but it can get tangled in knots.

What demands of one the compromise of
one's integrity or arrests the progression of one's
humanity is a form of corruption that *must
be avoided* if one is to remain faithful to
the higher calling.

To always be true, to always stand by one's
principles, one must be free (i.e., live with a
freedom that no human being can give to you,
but you).

The enlightened do not allow praise
of any kind to inflate their head nor
unwarranted blame to shrink their heart.

When you don't try to impress, don't try to
fit in, don't try to sell, don't try to convince,
a sincerity comes through that is irrefutable.

Maturity moves into the realm of the
spiritual when one no longer solicits
applause or adulation from others.

To step out of *the box* is to step out of
"personality."

Who does everything in the way it has
always been done lives a life in a manner
that was never meant to be.

Few errors are more common or made
with greater frequency than equating
rejection with failure, and acceptance
with success.

Each life is of a truth inimitable unto itself,
and harmonizing with Truth — (but only
when its truth is being lived).

Better to have Truth as a companion, though
vilified by the whole world, than to be without
Truth, though embraced by all the world.

Too precious is life and short in its time
for farce of any stripe.

What does a maintenance of the body's
health matter where the same is not done
for the soul.

Who don't live their lives in union
with the core of their being do nothing
authentic, because the root of their
activity is inauthentic.

One cannot hear the music of the
universe who has not heard (not felt)
the music within.

What is adopted of values or beliefs is
not enough to sustain one. Only what
evolves from within is of a power
that can nourish and sustain.

The rule of every substantive life is
self-creation, guided by the inner light.

Only those who belong to themselves
are capable of profound giving.

You must cultivate the life that is
your own if it is to bear fruit that
is uniquely its own.

With courage, sacrifice, discipline,
the life that is yours is won.

A gift or power cannot be fully
realized until it is used for what
it is meant for.

Sometimes fortunes are overlooked
so fortunes of a higher order may be
attained.

In the spiritual, one arrives at what one
has created.

A mastering of discipline is a continuity
of creative energy brought to the discipline.

What will yield for you the highest return
will always be what can be done by no other
than you — your inner work . . . (your
spiritual work).

The aim in the spiritual is as important
as the achievement.

Boundaries of a life may be increased
where persistence is faithfully present.

What is without challenge is without promise.

While on route to realizing their best the noble of spirit ensure that they do not obstruct others from doing the same.

Meditations are not essentially about one's peace and contentment if truly focused on the transcendent — they're about growing one's spirituality for the good of the world.

When free of greed and envy one is prepared
to live the most free and noble life a human
being is able to live.

The journey of enlightenment is toward
doing what is right to becoming what is right.

The cunnings of the world are too contrived,
too guileful for the ways of enlightenment, for
it embodies openness and directness, aiming
for justice and truth in all dealings with others.

Only the life of principle can achieve its ideals.

It is those who are willing to walk away from what many would consider to be an opportunity of a lifetime that are more likely to discover the treasure of an eternity.

Am I liked, am I loved, am I popular, am I respected, am I . . . am I . . . .? What does any of this matter when doing the work of one's life?

Every moment spent on trying to impress
is a spiritual regression.

To draw away from the hollow is to
make way for the welcoming of the
spiritually nourishing.

Moving up takes place in the mind,
heart and spirit. Nowhere else.

In the realm of the temporal, growth
is but an illusion.

Who does not know solitude cannot know
the full scope of where he's been wrong
and where he's been right in the motions
of his life.

There cannot be unity with Life
where there is not unity within.

The enlightened spirit lives passionately, but doesn't allow passions to take control of the reins.

Not to be put off balance when alone or in a crowd, not to be moved from one's center is to stay with what is higher . . . deeper . . .

With the purgation of frivolous wants from a life comes a burgeoning of possibilities for greater life.

Human life can be joyous in a spiritual sense
to the degree that it feels its strength, and can
feel its strength only so far as it is free from
enslavement to the fleeting.

The strongest of spirits are like Nature:
stoic, yet fiercely intense in their operations.

The more creative and complex the
activity, the simpler everyday living
must be.

Neither wise nor healthy is holding to
the tie that suffocates.

Even a small measure of misguided
ambition can deprive a life of much
goodness and truth.

Of even the longest of lives, time is not
sufficient to veer from the spiritual path.

Like foreign currency, spiritual wealth is
not recognized by the impoverished spirit.

Better to walk alone than with the brash,
the pompous, the arrogant, or the flatterer,
the yes-man, the sycophant.

Your life is depending on you to realize
its promise.

To be different is to invite ridicule, but it is also to invite the world to something new.

The best of merit is not a requirement to know the best of worldly offerings.

The road less travelled will ever yield the better fruit.

The path of enlightenment can be inimical
to earthly modes of comfort, for the jewels of
wisdom are not given to those who approach
slothfully, without commitment or sacrifice;
it does not cater to the pampered, the ones
who are looking for the easy, pain-free
journey in the spiritual quest as they want
and expect in their everyday lives.

Though more than truth is needed to
create inner depth, no such depth of
any measure can be created without it.

There is not treasure to speak of
throughout humankind whose
emanation is not from within.

Only by living through the inner light
can one bring light to the world.

How casual the phrase "get the most
out of life" passes through the lips of
many every day, when *give the most to
life* would be the more constructive
and noble motto to live by.

Much may lead astray, but nothing
more so than ego.

The in-crowd is ever out of range from where the real industry in human progress is taking place.

Ego makes it easy to accept the illusions of the temporal. It must therefore be shed if one is to see with greater clarity.

The larger the gathering the harder it is for truth to breathe.

Their way is lost who give way to the demands of the world rife with falsehood and banality.

The noble life is founded on the noble character.

Without inner work one is no more evolved spiritually at the age of seventy than at the age of twenty.

It is easy to be committed to growth
in an inspired moment; what counts
is the commitment for a lifetime.

The spiritual aspirant can live and
participate in the day-to-day, but cannot
make it central to his or her being
if they are to stay the call of the journey.

It is not possible to save time; one
can only spend it wisely.

The wise not only trim the fat out of their diets, but also out of their lives.

Values can be as harmful as toxins when accepted without thought or question

To be enlightened is to be as acutely aware of the darkness as of the light.

It is folly to assume that anything of the
fleeting could inspire a sense of purpose
beyond the fleeting.

The one noble ambition is that of wanting
to serve the spiritual of life. Ambitions
of the base are those that are grounded in
wanting to "get ahead" at any cost, trading
integrity for gains that never equal the trade.

By operations solely through animal nature
large sums of monetary wealth can be amassed,
but not one coin of the spiritual.

One has only so much time to discover
the timeless — (and when this is missed,
life is missed).

There is no such thing as a "healthy ego."

What is of the spiritual is all that can
nourish the spiritual.

Spirituality isn't just something to be studied, but something to be lived.

To live through the temporal is the same as living through a part and not the whole, living only in part.

There is a difference between a life that seeks reward, and the life that is rewarding.

A hand opening can never extend
longer or wider than when it is fully
open — and also the soul and heart.

Know that enlightenment cannot be
where generosity is not present.

It is through selflessness that
self-realization is attained.

No life is more blessed than one of a progressive strengthening of noble purpose.

As the swimmer cuts the water making an impact according to the strength of his or her body, so one moves one's life through the currents of existence, effecting an impact according to the strength of one's spirit.

It is wise to follow life's lead, always going forward, leaving yesterday behind.

Life of the eternal is of great responsibility, greater than all responsibilities of the temporal combined.

No matter how far one goes there is a duty to go further.

To do something with genuine love and conviction is to do it even if it would be that no one would ever see it, hear of it, or know of it but you.

In communications there is a point where the distance is too great for a signal to get through. So too the distance sometimes between those who embark on the spiritual journey and those who stay behind.

Whatever the journey's cost it cannot be near enough to pay for what is received in return.

Where you have been has everything to do with where you are now able to go.

One may be inspired by others, but
not moved from one stage of spiritual
growth to the next by another.

To work for what is hoped for is to
diminish the need for hope.

The obstacles are the best part of the
journey (but one must be well into
the journey for this to be recognized).

They are most fulfilled who are always
testing themselves, challenging themselves,
to do today what they had not dreamed of
doing yesterday.

The force of electricity is of no use to the
human race if it is not harnessed with intelligence.
Likewise, the powers of mind and spirit.

In Nature many a species requires two to
make one of its kind, but in the spiritual,
one can create many of multiple kinds.

Creativity is the spiritual blood of
Humankind. Without it nothing spiritual
can be realized or conceived.

Not all moments of a life need to
be fleeting — some may be eternal,
depending on what is done with them.

There is nothing in the universe more
powerful than creative energy. There is
also nothing more fragile.

There are searchers who earnestly seek
enlightenment, devoting years to the
exploration who one day desire to
create light but are only able to
generate heat, because they spent
too much time on the teachings of
others and not enough on creating
illuminations of their own.

When listening to the life-music of
another, whatever its beauty, never
neglect a music rising within you
(even if not as beautiful).

A single experience can be the spark
that sets off a deluge of creative thought
and insight. Such is the wonder and
potential of human life.

One is of the source that generates all,
but if an individuality is not created
with its power, one does an injustice
to one's life and dishonors the source
from which it comes.

The silence of solitude is like a quiet
stranger ever before one, waiting for
one's best.

If the soil is not turned, fresh harvest
cannot come forth. If a life is not
transformed, nothing of the spiritual
can grow.

The strengthening of the spirit should
be diligently engaged, for when its
bounty is ready for harvest, how will it
be gathered if one's spirit is not up to
the task?

To harden with strength one must first
soften with love.

What follows the annihilation of ego
is so much more than the sum of what
the ego had fashioned.

The greatest triumphs of a human life
go unnoticed. They are the triumphs
over the baser attributes of human
constitution — personal victories
without accolade or applause.

Not to monitor one's actions out
of fear of damnation, but love and
compassion . . . this, the way of the
noble spirit and heart.

The sense of duty that comes from
principle, i.e., that would be honored
regardless of compensation or reward,
is of nobility; never the action that
emanates from outside pressures,
compelled by fear or shame if what
one is expected to do is not done.

Present too is nobility in being
able to crush an ant but choosing
to walk around it.

To live in concert with enlightenment
is to live in a manner that never favors
the personal over the universal.

The primary mission of the spiritual
journey is not to arrive at a place for
oneself, but to help others on the way
in the many ways that this can be
accomplished.

When pondering the question "Why
am I here?" take a look around and see
what needs to be done, or if you can
be of service to anyone. It is there
you will find your answer.

Only in service and contribution can
human life be purposefully connected
to the everlasting.

To help is to love.

Who is not here to give of oneself
is not really *here* in the truer sense . . .
(in the spiritual sense).

The noble of spirit go through life
willing to help everyone, but realize
that not everyone will be helped, or
be open to what they have to give.
(Still, they go on giving.)

Many equate the soul too much
with death — what it will be for
them when their lives have passed
instead of what it can be for them
now, in this life . . . and *more
importantly*, what they can be
[can do] for the spiritual.

Life is a perennial test of what
one is made of and revelation of
where one is in the advance of
the principal journey.

How far one has travelled on the
spiritual path is gauged by the
inner work.

It is the most enlightened who are
always working toward greater light.

No further from the divine can anything
be than the closed mind and heart.

Even in times of great trial those who
live through the spiritual can be kind
and generous to others.

You enter the world by means other than
your own, a gift of various elements and
conditions giving you life. This gift is honored
when living your life in the spirit of giving.

With everything you do for others
you move deeper into yourself — (your
spiritual self).

The more one gives the larger one's
spirit grows.

It is through love that all avenues to
higher ground lie open.

The enlightened don't aim at selling themselves to the world, but at giving their best to life.

The question "Need I say more?" can often be answered with "No." The question "Need I do more?" can always be answered with "Yes."

Like taking the elasticity out of the rubber band would be taking the challenge out of life.

It is not the ones who are well
satisfied with the status quo, who
never think otherwise than it being
fine just as it is, that do what they
can to make things better. It is those
who say No, it isn't good enough, it
could be better, *must* be better —
and spend their lives doing what
they're able to improve of the world
what can be improved.

It requires many to sustain changes
that bear true benefit for humankind,
but only one to set a change in motion.

Waiting to be turned into reality
is the dream of aspiration.

A waning of inspiration . . . what
is its remedy? To draw closer to
the divine.

The divine is always with you,
within you, but to feel its presence
and know of its power, a consciousness
beyond the temporal must be achieved.

All productions of a profound nature
manifesting the spiritual bear the mark
of objectivity.

It is discipline that shapes inspiration,
and inspiration that maintains discipline.

The highest creations of Life speak
through the creations of the human
mind and spirit.

Greatness too has its rules that if
violated retreats from the soul in
which it has lived.

So much artifice, distraction, temptation
in the temporal promising only the false,
when truth stands ready to be received.

A bowl made out of glass may be exquisite
in design and appearance, but it will always
be a glass bowl, never china, silver or gold.

Where the "real action" is, or the best of
happenings are presumed to be taking place,
one will seldom find anything more than
the equivalent of decorated walls of
cardboard with nothing behind them.

Illusion leads to disillusionment.

In Life is where one needs to be.

One can never reach the mother lode
of one's true treasure if one spends
more time than one needs to on the
ever fading.

The modern aspirant must develop a perception his or her predecessors did not have — must adjust their sight to navigate through current times, yet still remain focused on what is beyond time.

An indifference to much that goes on in the world is a necessity if one is to make a difference.

A life of discipline is a regimen of dos and don'ts, of action and restraint.

The power of self-control is greater than any power one could have over others.

Who lives through the spiritual seeks what Life asks of him or her and asks for nothing in return, save for the privilege to serve.

They have not advanced beyond the superficial who perceive others as rivals and competitors rather than fellow travellers through life.

Enlightenment is not in striving to have more, but to be more.

The day leaves with most of what is said and done. All that remains of human life is endeavor in service of the spiritual.

Many assume worldly progress to be a linear progression, but in truth it is like a dog chasing its tail.

The wise stake nothing today on
what will not matter tomorrow.

When living through the ageless
there is no desire for the artificially
produced, for one is joined to what
is real, living for what is always.

An incessant preoccupation with the
fleeting is as detrimental to spiritual
health as a nutrition-starved diet
would be to physical health.

Every day there are those who sell
their bodies, and there are many
outcries of condemnation; and more
who sell their souls, and hardly a
whimper of condemnation.

A full life can be of no more substance
than an empty one if filled with error
and triviality.

There is something deep within the
core of spiritual-being that knows
instinctively what is important of
all there is and will be.

The prime function of a serious discipline is to achieve a state of inner charge where the many undisciplined happenings going on around one cannot disturb the work vital to the realization of what is higher.

Time for yourself is something you must give to yourself, for no one else is going to give it to you. (That is, time to develop so more may be given to others.)

What moves one to focus on a negative of one's life that is able to be corrected, is a positive.

What you overlook in the present
regarding your mission of growth is
sure to be looking at you some day
in the future.

True growth is a growing up, a growing
out, a growing in, a growing down . . . up
beyond animal nature into the realm of the
spiritual; out beyond the confines of ego-
interest into concern and consideration for
others; in to the core of inner being to a
developing of self-awareness and the
discovery of endowments and potentials,
and down into the depths of soul to face
the full of its power, accepting the
challenge of its miracle.

There is no shortcut to spiritual bliss.

There are "gurus" who address their
audience on what it is to be enlightened,
conveying the notion that a few easy steps
will get them there, giving the impression
that the measure of difficulty to achieve it
is near tantamount to spending some time
at a spa resort with a rich assortment of
candies and desserts and other pleasures
for the palate to enjoy, when what they'll
really need to do is down some spinach
and castor oil, so to speak (lots of it) in an
ambiance far less comfortable to come
close to the heart of enlightenment.

One can experience no greater trials
than on the principal [spiritual] journey,
but they are trials pregnant with the
greatest of joy.

It is trial that prepares one for the light.

Suffering does evil only when its gifts
are neglected or lessons are ignored.

The enlightened let no experience go to
waste as material for learning, and when
possible, creating.

Complete knowledge is unattainable,
but the unending quest to learn deepens
and expands the lives of those who
yearn to know.

Whatever the circumstance there is
benefit to be gleaned, for there is always
something to learn, and to learn is to
benefit.

When life slips into a minor key
one may fail to notice or appreciate
the value of its offering, and what it
has to teach.

To both sunlight and rain the flower
must open to bloom the entirety of
its beauty.

Greater than any wealth of the
material is the spiritual prosperity
born of adversity.

For those determined to find it (or
create it) there is a way out of . . .
a way into . . . where and when
it is needed.

Compassion and empathy for others
has the noble heart, but never an
indulgence of self-pity.

The benevolent need not speak of their goodness, the wise, of their enlightenment.

With true gratitude within, the gratitude of others is not necessary to always be open to helping them.

The world moves of its own accord, but into the motion one may contribute love or hatred, kindness or ill-will, a base selfishness or a noble generosity.

A rich life cannot be that is not one of
selfless giving.

Those who give everything not only bring
benefit to the lives of others, but also change
things for the better in their own lives to
great measure.

One cannot live well spiritually speaking
without the desire and commitment to
do well by others.

Among those who have walked in sandals and ragged clothes are ones who have given more to the world than those who rode on stallions in glowing armor and raised sword.

There is only one justification for wanting more, and that is to give more.

Ego is the jailer, humility, the liberator of human life.

Love is at the helm of all serious
contribution to the world.

When the last vestige of selfishness
exits a life, paradise enters.

The sun demonstrates that of the realm
of space and matter nothing belongs to
anyone, or everything belongs to everyone
to nourish and sustain life . . . and: does
the water rise up and rush away, or the fruit
flee from the tree, or the vegetable, from the
field or garden, when anyone comes to eat or
drink of their gifts? Be they male or female,
white, black, brown, yellow, or red? Be they
Buddhist, Christian, Jew, Muslim, or Hindu?

The realization of one's best can
never be without the acknowledgement,
encouragement and celebration of the
best of others with joy, free of all envy.

To reach a state of growth where ego
has been overcome is to be where it is
impossible to willfully do wrong.

It is the humblest of souls who hold
within their hearts the highest love.

No matter what leaves or falls, the
work of the spiritual needs to go on.

Follow in the direction of the wise
that have gone before you, but on
your own path.

Wherever you find yourself at any time
in your life, stay alert, for you are at a point
to perceive and assimilate peculiar to your
position, to see and experience what no other
can at that moment, if willing to engage the
moment . . . something to be absorbed that will
remain with you and continue to bring insight
and instruction to your life to one day return,
transformed into spiritual benefaction.

Let the world go its way when not
going yours, and have faith that all
you encounter is necessary to reveal
to you a deeper reality.

Debates have raged for centuries over
what is best for human life, which ideals
and principles should be embraced, what
dogma or ideology should be followed,
what values to live by; these debates will
continue to go on . . . let them — for truth
will always be on the side of what elevates
and endures, present in the achievement
of service that mortality cannot claim,
where shines the brightest light into the
darkness of fear and ignorance and brings
the greatest good to humankind, staying
forever beyond the bickering and clashing
interests of generation after generation,
like a dawn that never fades, lighting of
the eternal, untouched by time and place.

ABOUT THE AUTHOR

Carroll Blair is an author of more than twenty
books and the recipient of numerous awards.
His work has been well endorsed and com-
mendably reviewed. Among his titles cited
for distinction are *Through the Shadows*, winner
of the Pacific Book Awards, and *Quarter Notes*,
winner of the Sharp Writ Book Awards.
He is an alumnus of the Boston Conservatory
and lives in Massachusetts.

www.ingramcontent.com/pod-product-compliance
Lightning Source LLC
Chambersburg PA
CBHW021206020426
42331CB00003B/227